Setting Up

Podcast Name: _____

Tagline: _____

Niche: _____ Co-host (?): _____

Target Audience

-
-
-
-

_____
_____
_____
_____
_____

Cover Art

Hosting: _____

Domain Name: _____

Additional Information:

_____
_____
_____
_____
_____

Show Format

Length		Frequency of Episode Release	
Style			
Intro Music			
Outro Music			

Episode Format	Notes
●	
●	
●	
●	
●	
●	
●	
●	

Intro Podcast Script Template:

Outro Podcast Script Template:

Equipment & Software Log

No.	Type	Brand	Cost

Outsourcing

Type Of Service	Hiring Platform	Name of Freelancer/Company	Cost

Reach-Out

No.	People To Reach Out To	Purpose	Contact Information

Reach-Out

No.	People To Reach Out To	Purpose	Contact Information

Planning Ahead

Episode #	Topic Idea	Est Recording Date	Est Broadcast Date	Guest(s)

Planning Ahead

Episode #	Topic Idea	Est Recording Date	Est Broadcast Date	Guest(s)

Planning Ahead

Episode #	Topic Idea	Est Recording Date	Est Broadcast Date	Guest(s)

Planning Ahead

Episode #	Topic Idea	Est Recording Date	Est Broadcast Date	Guest(s)

Episode #	Recording Location:
Recording Date:	Broadcast Date:

Host(s) _____

Guest(s) _____ Fee(?) _____

Main Feature _____

Running Order

Time Stamp	Segment

Music / FX _____

Contest

Sponsor _____

Prize _____

Winner _____

Talking Points

_____

_____

_____

_____

_____

Checklist

- [ ] Edit recording
- [ ] Upload podcast
- [ ] Share podcast
- [ ] Create transcriptions /show notes

Script Notes

Episode #	Recording Location:
Recording Date:	Broadcast Date:

Host(s) _____

Guest(s) _____ Fee(?) _____

Main Feature _____

Running Order

Time Stamp	Segment

Music / FX _____

Contest

Sponsor _____

Prize _____

Winner _____

Talking Points

_____
_____
_____
_____
_____

Checklist

☐ Edit recording _____

☐ Upload podcast _____

☐ Share podcast _____

☐ Create _____
transcriptions _____
/show notes _____

Script Notes

_____

_____

_____

_____

_____

_____

_____

_____

_____

_____

_____

_____

_____

_____

_____

Episode #	Recording Location:
Recording Date:	Broadcast Date:

Host(s) _____

Guest(s) _____ Fee(?) _____

Main Feature _____

Running Order

Time Stamp	Segment

Music / FX _____

Contest

Sponsor _____

Prize _____

Winner _____

Talking Points

_____

_____

_____

_____

_____

Checklist

- ☐ Edit recording
- ☐ Upload podcast
- ☐ Share podcast
- ☐ Create transcriptions /show notes

Script Notes

Episode #	Recording Location:
Recording Date:	Broadcast Date:

Host(s) _____

Guest(s) _____ Fee(?) _____

Main Feature _____

Running Order

Time Stamp	Segment

Music / FX _____

Contest

Sponsor _____

Prize _____

Winner _____

Talking Points

_____

_____

_____

_____

_____

Checklist

- ☐ Edit recording _____
- ☐ Upload podcast _____
- ☐ Share podcast _____
- ☐ Create transcriptions /show notes _____

Script Notes

_____
_____
_____
_____
_____
_____
_____
_____
_____
_____
_____
_____
_____
_____
_____
_____

Episode #	Recording Location:
Recording Date:	Broadcast Date:

Host(s) _____

Guest(s) _____ Fee(?) _____

Main Feature _____

Running Order

Time Stamp	Segment

Music / FX _____

Contest

Sponsor _____

Prize _____

Winner _____

Talking Points

_____

_____

_____

_____

_____

_____

Checklist

- ☐ **Edit recording** _____
- ☐ **Upload podcast** _____
- ☐ **Share podcast** _____
- ☐ **Create transcriptions /show notes** _____

Script Notes

_____
_____
_____
_____
_____
_____
_____
_____
_____
_____
_____
_____
_____
_____

Episode #	Recording Location:
Recording Date:	Broadcast Date:

Host(s) _____

Guest(s) _____ Fee(?) _____

Main Feature _____

Running Order

Time Stamp	Segment

Music / FX _____

Contest

Sponsor _____

Prize _____

Winner _____

Talking Points

_____

_____

_____

_____

_____

Checklist

- [ ] **Edit recording** _____
- [ ] **Upload podcast** _____
- [ ] **Share podcast** _____
- [ ] **Create transcriptions /show notes** _____

Script Notes

_____

_____

_____

_____

_____

_____

_____

_____

_____

_____

_____

_____

_____

_____

_____

Episode #	Recording Location:
Recording Date:	Broadcast Date:

Host(s) _____

Guest(s) _____ Fee(?) _____

Main Feature _____

Running Order

Time Stamp	Segment

Music / FX _____

Contest

Sponsor _____

Prize _____

Winner _____

Talking Points

_____

_____

_____

_____

_____

Checklist

☐ Edit recording _____

☐ Upload podcast _____

☐ Share podcast _____

☐ Create
transcriptions _____
/show notes
_____

_____

Script Notes

_____

_____

_____

_____

_____

_____

_____

_____

_____

_____

_____

_____

_____

_____

_____

Episode #	Recording Location:
Recording Date:	Broadcast Date:

Host(s) _____

Guest(s) _____ Fee(?) _____

Main Feature _____

Running Order

Time Stamp	Segment

Music / FX _____

Contest

Sponsor _____

Prize _____

Winner _____

Talking Points

_____

_____

_____

_____

_____

Checklist

☐ Edit recording　　_____

☐ Upload podcast　　_____

☐ Share podcast　　_____

☐ Create
transcriptions
/show notes

_____

_____

_____

Script Notes

_____
_____
_____
_____
_____
_____
_____
_____
_____
_____
_____
_____
_____
_____
_____

Episode #	Recording Location:
Recording Date:	Broadcast Date:

Host(s) _____

Guest(s) _____ Fee(?) _____

Main Feature _____

Running Order

Time Stamp	Segment

Music / FX _____

Contest

Sponsor _____

Prize _____

Winner _____

Talking Points

_____

_____

_____

_____

_____

Checklist

- ☐ Edit recording   _____
- ☐ Upload podcast   _____
- ☐ Share podcast   _____
- ☐ Create transcriptions /show notes

_____

_____

_____

Script Notes

_____

_____

_____

_____

_____

_____

_____

_____

_____

_____

_____

_____

_____

_____

_____

Episode #	Recording Location:
Recording Date:	Broadcast Date:

Host(s) _____

Guest(s) _____ Fee(?) _____

Main Feature _____

Running Order

Time Stamp	Segment

Music / FX _____

Contest

Sponsor _____

Prize _____

Winner _____

Talking Points

_____

_____

_____

_____

_____

Checklist

☐   Edit recording

                      _____

☐   Upload podcast

                      _____

☐   Share podcast

                      _____

☐   Create
transcriptions
/show notes

Script Notes

Episode #	Recording Location:
Recording Date:	Broadcast Date:

Host(s) _____

Guest(s) _____ Fee(?) _____

Main Feature _____

Running Order

Time Stamp	Segment

Music / FX _____

Contest

Sponsor _____

Prize _____

Winner _____

Talking Points

_____

_____

_____

_____

_____

Checklist

- ☐ Edit recording _____
- ☐ Upload podcast _____
- ☐ Share podcast _____
- ☐ Create transcriptions /show notes _____

Script Notes

_____
_____
_____
_____
_____
_____
_____
_____
_____
_____
_____
_____
_____
_____
_____
_____

Episode #	Recording Location:
Recording Date:	Broadcast Date:

Host(s) _____

Guest(s) _____ Fee(?) _____

Main Feature _____

Running Order

Time Stamp	Segment

Music / FX _____

Contest

Sponsor _____

Prize _____

Winner _____

Talking Points

_____

_____

_____

_____

_____

Checklist

☐ Edit recording _____

☐ Upload podcast _____

☐ Share podcast _____

☐ Create
transcriptions _____
/show notes
_____

Script Notes

_____

_____

_____

_____

_____

_____

_____

_____

_____

_____

_____

_____

_____

_____

_____

Episode #	Recording Location:
Recording Date:	Broadcast Date:

Host(s) _____

Guest(s) _____ Fee(?) _____

Main Feature _____

Running Order

Time Stamp	Segment

Music / FX _____

Contest

Sponsor _____

Prize _____

Winner _____

Talking Points

_____

_____

_____

_____

_____

Checklist

☐ Edit recording

☐ Upload podcast

☐ Share podcast

☐ Create transcriptions /show notes

Script Notes

Episode #	Recording Location:
Recording Date:	Broadcast Date:

Host(s) _____

Guest(s) _____ Fee(?) _____

Main Feature _____

Running Order

Time Stamp	Segment

Music / FX _____

Contest

Sponsor _____

Prize _____

Winner _____

Talking Points

_____

_____

_____

_____

_____

Checklist

☐ Edit recording   _____

☐ Upload podcast   _____

☐ Share podcast   _____

☐ Create
transcriptions
/show notes

_____

_____

_____

Script Notes

_____

_____

_____

_____

_____

_____

_____

_____

_____

_____

_____

_____

_____

_____

Episode #	Recording Location:
Recording Date:	Broadcast Date:

Host(s) _____

Guest(s) _____ Fee(?) _____

Main Feature _____

Running Order

Time Stamp	Segment

Music / FX _____

Contest

Sponsor _____

Prize _____

Winner _____

Talking Points

_____

_____

_____

_____

_____

_____

Checklist

☐ **Edit recording** _____

☐ **Upload podcast** _____

☐ **Share podcast** _____

☐ **Create transcriptions /show notes** _____
_____

Script Notes

_____
_____
_____
_____
_____
_____
_____
_____
_____
_____
_____
_____
_____
_____
_____
_____

Episode #	Recording Location:
Recording Date:	Broadcast Date:

Host(s) _____

Guest(s) _____ Fee(?) _____

Main Feature _____

Running Order

Time Stamp	Segment

Music / FX _____

Contest

Sponsor _____

Prize _____

Winner _____

Talking Points

_____

_____

_____

_____

_____

Checklist

- ☐ Edit recording _____
- ☐ Upload podcast _____
- ☐ Share podcast _____
- ☐ Create transcriptions /show notes

_____

_____

_____

Script Notes

_____

_____

_____

_____

_____

_____

_____

_____

_____

_____

_____

_____

_____

_____

Episode #	Recording Location:
Recording Date:	Broadcast Date:

Host(s) _____

Guest(s) _____ Fee(?) _____

Main Feature _____

Running Order

Time Stamp	Segment

Music / FX _____

Contest

Sponsor _____

Prize _____

Winner _____

Talking Points

_____

_____

_____

_____

_____

Checklist

☐ Edit recording _____

☐ Upload podcast _____

☐ Share podcast _____

☐ Create transcriptions /show notes _____
_____

Script Notes

_____
_____
_____
_____
_____
_____
_____
_____
_____
_____
_____
_____
_____
_____
_____
_____

Episode #	Recording Location:
Recording Date:	Broadcast Date:

Host(s) _____

Guest(s) _____ Fee(?) _____

Main Feature _____

Running Order

Time Stamp	Segment

Music / FX _____

Contest

Sponsor _____

Prize _____

Winner _____

Talking Points

_____

_____

_____

_____

_____

Checklist

☐ Edit recording   _____

☐ Upload podcast   _____

☐ Share podcast   _____

☐ Create transcriptions /show notes

_____

_____

_____

Script Notes

_____

_____

_____

_____

_____

_____

_____

_____

_____

_____

_____

_____

_____

_____

_____

Episode #	Recording Location:
Recording Date:	Broadcast Date:

Host(s) _____

Guest(s) _____ Fee(?) _____

Main Feature _____

Running Order

Time Stamp	Segment

Music / FX _____

Contest

Sponsor _____

Prize _____

Winner _____

Talking Points

_____

_____

_____

_____

_____

Checklist

☐ Edit recording   _____

☐ Upload podcast   _____

☐ Share podcast   _____

☐ Create
transcriptions   _____
/show notes
  _____

  _____

Script Notes

_____

_____

_____

_____

_____

_____

_____

_____

_____

_____

_____

_____

_____

_____

_____

Episode #	Recording Location:
Recording Date:	Broadcast Date:

Host(s) _____

Guest(s) _____ Fee(?) _____

Main Feature _____

Running Order

Time Stamp	Segment

Music / FX _____

Contest

Sponsor _____

Prize _____

Winner _____

Talking Points

_____

_____

_____

_____

_____

Checklist

- ☐ Edit recording
- ☐ Upload podcast
- ☐ Share podcast
- ☐ Create transcriptions /show notes

Script Notes

Episode #	Recording Location:
Recording Date:	Broadcast Date:

Host(s) _____

Guest(s) _____ Fee(?) _____

Main Feature _____

Running Order

Time Stamp	Segment

Music / FX _____

Contest

Sponsor _____

Prize _____

Winner _____

Talking Points

_____

_____

_____

_____

_____

Checklist

☐ Edit recording

☐ Upload podcast

☐ Share podcast

☐ Create
transcriptions
/show notes

Script Notes

Episode #	Recording Location:
Recording Date:	Broadcast Date:

Host(s) _____

Guest(s) _____ Fee(?) _____

Main Feature _____

Running Order

Time Stamp	Segment

Music / FX _____

Contest

Sponsor _____

Prize _____

Winner _____

Talking Points

_____

_____

_____

_____

_____

_____

Checklist

☐ **Edit recording** _____

☐ **Upload podcast** _____

☐ **Share podcast** _____

☐ **Create transcriptions /show notes** _____

Script Notes

_____
_____
_____
_____
_____
_____
_____
_____
_____
_____
_____
_____
_____
_____
_____

Episode #	Recording Location:
Recording Date:	Broadcast Date:

Host(s) _____

Guest(s) _____ Fee(?) _____

Main Feature _____

Running Order

Time Stamp	Segment

Music / FX _____

Contest

Sponsor _____

Prize _____

Winner _____

Talking Points

_____

_____

_____

_____

_____

Checklist

☐ Edit recording   _____

☐ Upload podcast   _____

☐ Share podcast   _____

☐ Create   _____
transcriptions   _____
/show notes   _____

Script Notes

_____

_____

_____

_____

_____

_____

_____

_____

_____

_____

_____

_____

_____

_____

_____

_____

Episode #	Recording Location:
Recording Date:	Broadcast Date:

Host(s) _____

Guest(s) _____ Fee(?) _____

Main Feature _____

Running Order

Time Stamp	Segment

Music / FX _____

Contest

Sponsor _____

Prize _____

Winner _____

Talking Points

_____

_____

_____

_____

_____

_____

Checklist

☐ Edit recording   _____

☐ Upload podcast   _____

☐ Share podcast   _____

☐ Create
   transcriptions   _____
   /show notes

  _____

Script Notes

_____

_____

_____

_____

_____

_____

_____

_____

_____

_____

_____

_____

_____

_____

_____

Episode #	Recording Location:
Recording Date:	Broadcast Date:

Host(s) _____

Guest(s) _____ Fee(?) _____

Main Feature _____

Running Order

Time Stamp	Segment

Music / FX _____

Contest

Sponsor _____

Prize _____

Winner _____

Talking Points

_____

_____

_____

_____

_____

Checklist

- ☐ Edit recording _____

- ☐ Upload podcast _____

- ☐ Share podcast _____

- ☐ Create _____
  transcriptions
  /show notes _____

  _____

Script Notes

_____

_____

_____

_____

_____

_____

_____

_____

_____

_____

_____

_____

_____

_____

_____

_____

Episode #	Recording Location:
Recording Date:	Broadcast Date:

Host(s) _____

Guest(s) _____ Fee(?) _____

Main Feature _____

Running Order

Time Stamp	Segment

Music / FX _____

Contest

Sponsor _____

Prize _____

Winner _____

Talking Points

_____

_____

_____

_____

_____

Checklist

☐ Edit recording _____

☐ Upload podcast _____

☐ Share podcast _____

☐ Create _____
transcriptions
/show notes _____

_____

Script Notes

_____

_____

_____

_____

_____

_____

_____

_____

_____

_____

_____

_____

_____

_____

_____

_____

Episode #	Recording Location:
Recording Date:	Broadcast Date:

Host(s) _____

Guest(s) _____ Fee(?) _____

Main Feature _____

Running Order

Time Stamp	Segment

Music / FX _____

Contest

Sponsor _____

Prize _____

Winner _____

Talking Points

_____

_____

_____

_____

_____

Checklist

☐ Edit recording

☐ Upload podcast

☐ Share podcast

☐ Create
transcriptions
/show notes

Script Notes

Episode #	Recording Location:
Recording Date:	Broadcast Date:

Host(s) _____

Guest(s) _____ Fee(?) _____

Main Feature _____

Running Order

Time Stamp	Segment

Music / FX _____

Contest

Sponsor _____

Prize _____

Winner _____

Talking Points

_____

_____

_____

_____

_____

Checklist

☐ Edit recording _____

☐ Upload podcast _____

☐ Share podcast _____

☐ Create
transcriptions _____
/show notes
_____

_____

Script Notes

_____

_____

_____

_____

_____

_____

_____

_____

_____

_____

_____

_____

_____

_____

_____

Episode #	Recording Location:
Recording Date:	Broadcast Date:

Host(s) _____

Guest(s) _____ Fee(?) _____

Main Feature _____

Running Order

Time Stamp	Segment

Music / FX _____

Contest

Sponsor _____

Prize _____

Winner _____

Talking Points

_____

_____

_____

_____

_____

Checklist

☐ Edit recording

_____

☐ Upload podcast

_____

☐ Share podcast

_____

☐ Create
transcriptions
/show notes

_____

_____

_____

Script Notes

_____

_____

_____

_____

_____

_____

_____

_____

_____

_____

_____

_____

_____

_____

Episode #	Recording Location:
Recording Date:	Broadcast Date:

Host(s) _____

Guest(s) _____ Fee(?) _____

Main Feature _____

Running Order

Time Stamp	Segment

Music / FX _____

Contest

Sponsor _____

Prize _____

Winner _____

Talking Points

_____

_____

_____

_____

_____

Checklist

☐ Edit recording _____

☐ Upload podcast _____

☐ Share podcast _____

☐ Create
transcriptions _____
/show notes _____

_____

Script Notes

_____
_____
_____
_____
_____
_____
_____
_____
_____
_____
_____
_____
_____
_____
_____
_____

Episode #	Recording Location:
Recording Date:	Broadcast Date:

Host(s) _____

Guest(s) _____ Fee(?) _____

Main Feature _____

Running Order

Time Stamp	Segment

Music / FX _____

Contest

Sponsor _____

Prize _____

Winner _____

Talking Points

_____

_____

_____

_____

_____

Checklist

☐ Edit recording _____

☐ Upload podcast _____

☐ Share podcast _____

☐ Create _____
transcriptions
/show notes _____

_____

Script Notes

_____
_____
_____
_____
_____
_____
_____
_____
_____
_____
_____
_____
_____
_____
_____

Episode #	Recording Location:
Recording Date:	Broadcast Date:

Host(s) _____

Guest(s) _____ Fee(?) _____

Main Feature _____

Running Order

Time Stamp	Segment

Music / FX _____

Contest

Sponsor _____

Prize _____

Winner _____

Talking Points

_____

_____

_____

_____

_____

Checklist

☐ Edit recording

_____

☐ Upload podcast

_____

☐ Share podcast

_____

☐ Create
transcriptions
/show notes

_____

_____

_____

Script Notes

_____

_____

_____

_____

_____

_____

_____

_____

_____

_____

_____

_____

_____

_____

_____

Episode #	Recording Location:
Recording Date:	Broadcast Date:

Host(s) _____

Guest(s) _____ Fee(?) _____

Main Feature _____

Running Order

Time Stamp	Segment

Music / FX _____

Contest

Sponsor _____

Prize _____

Winner _____

Talking Points

_____

_____

_____

_____

_____

_____

Checklist

- ☐ Edit recording   _____
- ☐ Upload podcast   _____
- ☐ Share podcast   _____
- ☐ Create transcriptions /show notes

_____

_____

_____

Script Notes

_____

_____

_____

_____

_____

_____

_____

_____

_____

_____

_____

_____

_____

_____

_____

Episode #	Recording Location:
Recording Date:	Broadcast Date:

Host(s) _____

Guest(s) _____ Fee(?) _____

Main Feature _____

Running Order

Time Stamp	Segment

Music / FX _____

Contest

Sponsor _____

Prize _____

Winner _____

Talking Points

_____

_____

_____

_____

_____

Checklist

- [ ] Edit recording
- [ ] Upload podcast
- [ ] Share podcast
- [ ] Create transcriptions /show notes

Script Notes

Episode #	Recording Location:
Recording Date:	Broadcast Date:

Host(s) _____

Guest(s) _____ Fee(?) _____

Main Feature _____

Running Order

Time Stamp	Segment

Music / FX _____

Contest

Sponsor _____

Prize _____

Winner _____

Talking Points

_____

_____

_____

_____

_____

Checklist

☐ Edit recording _____

☐ Upload podcast _____

☐ Share podcast _____

☐ Create _____
  transcriptions
  /show notes _____

_____

Script Notes

_____

_____

_____

_____

_____

_____

_____

_____

_____

_____

_____

_____

_____

_____

_____

_____

_____

Episode #	Recording Location:
Recording Date:	Broadcast Date:

Host(s) _____

Guest(s) _____ Fee(?) _____

Main Feature _____

Running Order

Time Stamp	Segment

Music / FX _____

Contest

Sponsor _____

Prize _____

Winner _____

Talking Points

_____

_____

_____

_____

_____

Checklist

☐ Edit recording   _____

☐ Upload podcast   _____

☐ Share podcast   _____

☐ Create
    transcriptions   _____
    /show notes   _____
                     _____

Script Notes

_____

_____

_____

_____

_____

_____

_____

_____

_____

_____

_____

_____

_____

_____

_____

_____

Episode #	Recording Location:
Recording Date:	Broadcast Date:

Host(s) _____

Guest(s) _____ Fee(?) _____

Main Feature _____

Running Order

Time Stamp	Segment

Music / FX _____

Contest

Sponsor _____

Prize _____

Winner _____

Talking Points

_____

_____

_____

_____

_____

Checklist

☐ Edit recording _____

☐ Upload podcast _____

☐ Share podcast _____

☐ Create _____
transcriptions _____
/show notes _____

Script Notes

_____
_____
_____
_____
_____
_____
_____
_____
_____
_____
_____
_____
_____
_____
_____

Episode #	Recording Location:
Recording Date:	Broadcast Date:

Host(s) _____

Guest(s) _____ Fee(?) _____

Main Feature _____

Running Order

Time Stamp	Segment

Music / FX _____

Contest

Sponsor _____

Prize _____

Winner _____

Talking Points

_____

_____

_____

_____

_____

_____

Checklist

☐ Edit recording _____

☐ Upload podcast _____

☐ Share podcast _____

☐ Create
transcriptions _____
/show notes _____

_____

Script Notes

_____
_____
_____
_____
_____
_____
_____
_____
_____
_____
_____
_____
_____
_____
_____

Episode #	Recording Location:
Recording Date:	Broadcast Date:

Host(s) _____

Guest(s) _____ Fee(?) _____

Main Feature _____

Running Order

Time Stamp	Segment

Music / FX _____

Contest

Sponsor _____

Prize _____

Winner _____

Talking Points

_____

_____

_____

_____

_____

Checklist

☐ Edit recording _____

☐ Upload podcast _____

☐ Share podcast _____

☐ Create
transcriptions
/show notes _____

Script Notes

_____
_____
_____
_____
_____
_____
_____
_____
_____
_____
_____
_____
_____
_____

Episode #	Recording Location:
Recording Date:	Broadcast Date:

Host(s) _____

Guest(s) _____ Fee(?) _____

Main Feature _____

Running Order

Time Stamp	Segment

Music / FX _____

Contest

Sponsor _____

Prize _____

Winner _____

Talking Points

_____

_____

_____

_____

_____

Checklist

☐ **Edit recording**

_____

☐ **Upload podcast**

_____

☐ **Share podcast**

_____

☐ **Create transcriptions /show notes**

_____

_____

_____

Script Notes

_____

_____

_____

_____

_____

_____

_____

_____

_____

_____

_____

_____

_____

_____

_____

Episode #	Recording Location:
Recording Date:	Broadcast Date:

Host(s) _____

Guest(s) _____ Fee(?) _____

Main Feature _____

Running Order

Time Stamp	Segment

Music / FX _____

Contest

Sponsor _____

Prize _____

Winner _____

Talking Points

_____

_____

_____

_____

_____

Checklist

☐ **Edit recording** _____

☐ **Upload podcast** _____

☐ **Share podcast** _____

☐ **Create** _____
  transcriptions _____
  /show notes _____

Script Notes

_____

_____

_____

_____

_____

_____

_____

_____

_____

_____

_____

_____

_____

_____

_____

Episode #	Recording Location:
Recording Date:	Broadcast Date:

Host(s) _____

Guest(s) _____ Fee(?) _____

Main Feature _____

Running Order

Time Stamp	Segment

Music / FX _____

Contest

Sponsor _____

Prize _____

Winner _____

Talking Points

_____

_____

_____

_____

_____

Checklist

☐ Edit recording

    _____

☐ Upload podcast

    _____

☐ Share podcast

    _____

☐ Create
   transcriptions
   /show notes

    _____

    _____

    _____

Script Notes

_____

_____

_____

_____

_____

_____

_____

_____

_____

_____

_____

_____

_____

_____

_____

Episode #	Recording Location:
Recording Date:	Broadcast Date:

Host(s) _____

Guest(s) _____ Fee(?) _____

Main Feature _____

Running Order

Time Stamp	Segment

Music / FX _____

Contest

Sponsor _____

Prize _____

Winner _____

Talking Points

_____

_____

_____

_____

_____

_____

Checklist

☐ Edit recording _____

☐ Upload podcast _____

☐ Share podcast _____

☐ Create
transcriptions _____
/show notes
_____

_____

Script Notes

_____
_____
_____
_____
_____
_____
_____
_____
_____
_____
_____
_____
_____
_____
_____

Episode #	Recording Location:
Recording Date:	Broadcast Date:

Host(s) _____

Guest(s) _____ Fee(?) _____

Main Feature _____

Running Order

Time Stamp	Segment

Music / FX _____

Contest

Sponsor _____

Prize _____

Winner _____

Talking Points

_____

_____

_____

_____

_____

Checklist

☐ **Edit recording** _____

☐ **Upload podcast** _____

☐ **Share podcast** _____

☐ **Create transcriptions /show notes** _____

_____

_____

Script Notes

_____

_____

_____

_____

_____

_____

_____

_____

_____

_____

_____

_____

_____

_____

Episode #	Recording Location:
Recording Date:	Broadcast Date:

Host(s) _____

Guest(s) _____ Fee(?) _____

Main Feature _____

Running Order

Time Stamp	Segment

Music / FX _____

Contest

Sponsor _____

Prize _____

Winner _____

Talking Points

_____

_____

_____

_____

_____

Checklist

☐ Edit recording   _____

☐ Upload podcast   _____

☐ Share podcast   _____

☐ Create
   transcriptions   _____
   /show notes   _____

                                      _____

Script Notes

Episode #	Recording Location:
Recording Date:	Broadcast Date:

Host(s) _____

Guest(s) _____ Fee(?) _____

Main Feature _____

Running Order

Time Stamp	Segment

Music / FX _____

Contest

Sponsor _____

Prize _____

Winner _____

Talking Points

_____

_____

_____

_____

_____

Checklist

☐ Edit recording

☐ Upload podcast

☐ Share podcast

☐ Create transcriptions /show notes

Script Notes

Episode #	Recording Location:
Recording Date:	Broadcast Date:

Host(s) _____

Guest(s) _____ Fee(?) _____

Main Feature _____

Running Order

Time Stamp	Segment

Music / FX _____

Contest

Sponsor _____

Prize _____

Winner _____

Talking Points

_____

_____

_____

_____

_____

Checklist

☐ Edit recording   ————————————————————

☐ Upload podcast   ————————————————————

☐ Share podcast   ————————————————————

☐ Create
   transcriptions ————————————————————
   /show notes   ————————————————————

                  ————————————————————

Script Notes

Episode #	Recording Location:
Recording Date:	Broadcast Date:

Host(s) _____

Guest(s) _____ Fee(?) _____

Main Feature _____

Running Order

Time Stamp	Segment

Music / FX _____

Contest

Sponsor _____

Prize _____

Winner _____

Talking Points

_____

_____

_____

_____

_____

_____

Checklist

☐ Edit recording

☐ Upload podcast

☐ Share podcast

☐ Create
transcriptions
/show notes

Script Notes

Episode #	Recording Location:
Recording Date:	Broadcast Date:

Host(s) _____

Guest(s) _____ Fee(?) _____

Main Feature _____

Running Order

Time Stamp	Segment

Music / FX _____

Contest

Sponsor _____

Prize _____

Winner _____

Talking Points

_____

_____

_____

_____

_____

Checklist

☐ **Edit recording** _____

☐ **Upload podcast** _____

☐ **Share podcast** _____

☐ **Create transcriptions /show notes** _____
_____
_____

Script Notes

_____
_____
_____
_____
_____
_____
_____
_____
_____
_____
_____
_____
_____
_____
_____
_____

Episode #	Recording Location:
Recording Date:	Broadcast Date:

Host(s) _____

Guest(s) _____ Fee(?) _____

Main Feature _____

Running Order

Time Stamp	Segment

Music / FX _____

Contest

Sponsor _____

Prize _____

Winner _____

Talking Points

_____

_____

_____

_____

_____

Checklist

☐ Edit recording   _____

☐ Upload podcast   _____

☐ Share podcast   _____

☐ Create   _____
   transcriptions   _____
   /show notes   _____

Script Notes

Episode #	Recording Location:
Recording Date:	Broadcast Date:

Host(s) _____

Guest(s) _____ Fee(?) _____

Main Feature _____

Running Order

Time Stamp	Segment

Music / FX _____

Contest

Sponsor _____

Prize _____

Winner _____

Talking Points

_____

_____

_____

_____

_____

_____

Checklist

☐ Edit recording _____

☐ Upload podcast _____

☐ Share podcast _____

☐ Create _____
  transcriptions _____
  /show notes _____

Script Notes

_____
_____
_____
_____
_____
_____
_____
_____
_____
_____
_____
_____
_____
_____
_____
_____

Episode #	Recording Location:
Recording Date:	Broadcast Date:

Host(s) _____

Guest(s) _____ Fee(?) _____

Main Feature _____

Running Order

Time Stamp	Segment

Music / FX _____

Contest

Sponsor _____

Prize _____

Winner _____

Talking Points

_____

_____

_____

_____

_____

Checklist

- ☐ Edit recording

- ☐ Upload podcast

- ☐ Share podcast

- ☐ Create transcriptions /show notes

Script Notes

Episode #	Recording Location:
Recording Date:	Broadcast Date:

Host(s) _____

Guest(s) _____ Fee(?) _____

Main Feature _____

Running Order

Time Stamp	Segment

Music / FX _____

Contest

Sponsor _____

Prize _____

Winner _____

Talking Points

_____
_____
_____
_____
_____

Checklist

☐ **Edit recording** _____

☐ **Upload podcast** _____

☐ **Share podcast** _____

☐ **Create
transcriptions
/show notes** _____

Script Notes

_____
_____
_____
_____
_____
_____
_____
_____
_____
_____
_____
_____
_____
_____
_____
_____

Episode #	Recording Location:
Recording Date:	Broadcast Date:

Host(s) _____

Guest(s) _____ Fee(?) _____

Main Feature _____

Running Order

Time Stamp	Segment

Music / FX _____

Contest

Sponsor _____

Prize _____

Winner _____

Talking Points

_____

_____

_____

_____

_____

Checklist

☐ Edit recording _____

☐ Upload podcast _____

☐ Share podcast _____

☐ Create
  transcriptions _____
  /show notes
  _____

Script Notes

_____

_____

_____

_____

_____

_____

_____

_____

_____

_____

_____

_____

_____

_____

_____

_____

Episode #	Recording Location:
Recording Date:	Broadcast Date:

Host(s) _____

Guest(s) _____ Fee(?) _____

Main Feature _____

Running Order

Time Stamp	Segment

Music / FX _____

Contest

Sponsor _____

Prize _____

Winner _____

Talking Points

_____
_____
_____
_____
_____
_____

Checklist

☐ Edit recording _____

☐ Upload podcast _____

☐ Share podcast _____

☐ Create
transcriptions _____
/show notes
_____

_____

Script Notes

_____

_____

_____

_____

_____

_____

_____

_____

_____

_____

_____

_____

_____

_____

_____

_____

Episode #	Recording Location:
Recording Date:	Broadcast Date:

Host(s) _____

Guest(s) _____ Fee(?) _____

Main Feature _____

Running Order

Time Stamp	Segment

Music / FX _____

Contest

Sponsor _____

Prize _____

Winner _____

Talking Points

_____

_____

_____

_____

_____

_____

Checklist

☐ Edit recording

☐ Upload podcast

☐ Share podcast

☐ Create
  transcriptions
  /show notes

Script Notes

Episode #	Recording Location:
Recording Date:	Broadcast Date:

Host(s) _____

Guest(s) _____ Fee(?) _____

Main Feature _____

Running Order

Time Stamp	Segment

Music / FX _____

Contest

Sponsor _____

Prize _____

Winner _____

Talking Points

_____

_____

_____

_____

_____

Checklist

☐ Edit recording _____

☐ Upload podcast _____

☐ Share podcast _____

☐ Create
transcriptions _____
/show notes
_____

_____

Script Notes

_____

_____

_____

_____

_____

_____

_____

_____

_____

_____

_____

_____

_____

_____

_____

_____

_____

Episode #	Recording Location:
Recording Date:	Broadcast Date:

Host(s) _____

Guest(s) _____ Fee(?) _____

Main Feature _____

Running Order

Time Stamp	Segment

Music / FX _____

Contest

Sponsor _____

Prize _____

Winner _____

Talking Points

_____

_____

_____

_____

_____

_____

Checklist

☐ Edit recording _____

☐ Upload podcast _____

☐ Share podcast _____

☐ Create
transcriptions _____
/show notes
_____

_____

Script Notes

_____

_____

_____

_____

_____

_____

_____

_____

_____

_____

_____

_____

_____

_____

_____

_____

_____

Episode #	Recording Location:
Recording Date:	Broadcast Date:

Host(s) _____

Guest(s) _____ Fee(?) _____

Main Feature _____

Running Order

Time Stamp	Segment

Music / FX _____

Contest

Sponsor _____

Prize _____

Winner _____

Talking Points

_____

_____

_____

_____

_____

Checklist

☐ Edit recording   _____

☐ Upload podcast   _____

☐ Share podcast   _____

☐ Create
    transcriptions   _____
    /show notes

Script Notes

_____

_____

_____

_____

_____

_____

_____

_____

_____

_____

_____

_____

_____

_____

_____

_____

| Episode # | Recording Location: |
| Recording Date: | Broadcast Date: |

Host(s) _____

Guest(s) _____ Fee(?) _____

Main Feature _____

Running Order

Time Stamp	Segment

Music / FX _____

Contest

Sponsor _____

Prize _____

Winner _____

Talking Points

_____

_____

_____

_____

_____

Checklist

☐ Edit recording

_____

☐ Upload podcast

_____

☐ Share podcast

_____

☐ Create
transcriptions
/show notes

_____

_____

_____

Script Notes

_____
_____
_____
_____
_____
_____
_____
_____
_____
_____
_____
_____
_____
_____
_____
_____

Made in the USA
Lexington, KY
19 December 2019